esprit d´espresso

esprit d´espresso

A Guide To Making
and Enjoying Espresso
and Cappuccino at Home.

ROLF CORNELL

STEVEN SULLIVAN

dustro
PUBLISHING

First Published in Great Britain 1991.

Copyright © 1991 Rolf Cornell, Steven Sullivan, David Sullivan,
Dastro Publishing Ltd. 16 Bull Lane, London N18 1SX.

All Rights Reserved

ISBN 0-9518748-0-2

ACKNOWLEDGEMENTS

The authors would like to thank everyone involved with the production of this publication, and gratefully acknowledge the generous assistance and advice extended by David Sullivan of Dastro Publishing, who also contributed some of the recipes and took part in the many tasting sessions - Michael Zur-Szpiro of 'Aroma' for his support and continued encouragement, John Russell Storey of Lavazza UK Ltd for generously providing the coffee for the photography and recipe checks, Louie Salvoni, Andy Pugh and Geoff Pugh of Brasilia UK for the loan of espresso equipment, Eva Inzani of Brasilia for the translations of various Italian brochures, Dr David Goodson for lending the props on page 59 & 63, Patrician Antiques, Camden Passage, for the props on page 57, Bess Goodson for the props on Page 49, and finally, thanks to Sarah Sullivan for sourcing the newspapers for pages 43 and 51.

CREDITS

Concept, Recipes and Anecdotes –   *Steven Sullivan*

Photography, Set Design, Scenery and Model making,
Esprit d'Espresso Part One and Editing –   *Rolf Cornell*

Food Styling, Props and Sourcing –   *Anne Cornell, Steven Sullivan*

Line Drawings –   *Shaun West*

Book Design and Production –   *SCL Design, London*

Typesetting –   *Creative Pages, London*

Reproduction, Printing
and Binding –   *Splash Offset Litho Ltd., London*

THIS
PUBLICATION
IS DEDICATED
TO ALL
WHO STILL MAINTAIN
THE SIMPLE
ENJOYMENT
OF REAL
ROAST AND GROUND
COFFEE.

CONTENTS

esprit d´espresso

Part One
The Espresso Method

With virtually every Italian espresso-machine manufacturer having claimed for themselves the credit for originating the espresso system, at one time or another, much of which has always been misconstrued, it will probably come as a bit of a surprise to learn that the machine and method was originated by the Frenchman, one *Louis Bernard Rabaut*, as long ago as 1822, a fact the Italians prefer not to talk about.

The principle, based upon the machine, of heating the water to boiling inside a tank and letting steam gather at the top of the tank, then forcing the hot water through a straining device, containing the coffee, once a valve was opened below the water-surface, was the same as that employed by the oldest café machines and that of the present day home espresso brewers or stove-pots.

The idea was first put to commercial use by another Frenchman, *Edward Loysel de Santais*, some 21 years later. He produced a large café version which was subsequently shown to the world during the 1855 Paris Exposition. By the turn of the century, thankfully, a few Italians modified Santais's machine. Essentially they reduced the size of the strainer and increased the number of valves, to enable the brewing of several cups of coffee at the same time, rather than a pot at a time, drastically speeding up the procedure. It was this, the speed of the operation that coined the term of espresso.

The Italians took to the method with a great passion and it is now generally acknowledged that the modern café machine and caffè espresso method should be accredited to *Luigi Bezzera*, who in 1902 patented the first machine. His company, now run by his great grandson, *Guido Bezzera*, still manufacture and export world-wide their present day versions of the espresso machine.

What is espresso?

Most dictionaries quote the definition; "Pressed out coffee; coffee brewed by forcing steam through finely ground, darkly roasted coffee beans."

Technically this is somewhat incorrect. A more apt description should be as follows:

A concentrated coffee liqueur, between 1.5 and 2 fluid ounces, made by forcing water at a temperature of between 93°C and 96°C with a pressure of 9bar, through a tightly compacted 'wad' of finely ground, dark roasted coffee of between 6-7 grammes in weight, per portion, and a brewing duration of between 20-25 seconds.

The operation of the method is much cherished by the Italians, as they enact the ritual of ordering, brewing then drinking the coffee. It is this ritual which has gained popularity in many other countries, and the last ten years has seen a significant increase of espresso availability, world-wide, with even the Far East coming in on the act.

In Britain, the concept is much favoured, mainly because espresso also forms the basis for another Italian drink, the cappuccino, which fulfils with perfection the nation's tendency towards a milky beverage. The expression for cappuccino derives from its likeness in colour to that of the habit, worn by Capuchin monks. Whilst the British regard the drink as suitable at any time of the day, the Italian devotion to cappuccino ends with their breakfast.

Although the espresso concept came to Britain in the late 50's, when espresso bars became trendy places for the youth at that time, who perceived it as a kind of rebellion against their tea-drinking parents, its fashionable image, eventually, also caused its downfall. Films like *Espresso Bongo*, starring Cliff Richard, were made at the height of the boom, but due to the influence from their American counterparts, at a time when instant coffee was deemed to be 'hip' and with the Americans always portrayed drinking it, the British youngsters soon followed suite, and there ended the espresso phase of the 50's and 60's.

European travel, experiencing the drink in Italy, France or Spain, the general expectancy of higher food standards and a stronger taste requirement, collectively have contributed much to the public demanding as well as expecting this style of coffee, to generate once again, at least for Britain, the renaissance of espresso cuisine.

Louie Salvoni

The coffee world would have lost out, had it not been for the Italians and their continued development, tradition and faithfulness to coffee matters and to espresso cuisine in particular. *Caffè Espresso* encompasses several things all at once. It combines an aura of exclusivity, or at least an atmosphere as unique as the method of brewing it has contributed, with an aesthetic encounter all of its own, for those devoted to dining with it.

Responsible for perpetuating the sense of mystique, on one side and apprehension on the other, in part have been the technique for heating the milk (*Cappuccino*), brewing the coffee by forcing hot water under pressure through tightly packed coffee, a cup at a time, and the success of the resulting drink being largely due to that shiny, stylish monster of a machine, at home in many a European-style café, as well as due to the skill of the operator in accomplishing both, the right presentation and the right taste.

The advantage of espresso over other brewing methods, using roast and ground coffee, is the speed and efficiency with which the drink is made, essentially brewing the coffee under pressure rather than by gravity where the coffee is brewed in advance and allowed to sit. To magnify then the importance of the espresso system; - the pressurised water is forced through the coffee, making contact with every grain in no more than an instant, ensuring ultimate freshness, full flavour and aroma, and only the instant before you drink it. The less time hot water stays in contact with ground coffee, the less of those unpleasantly harsh and less soluble chemicals, natural to coffee, will be extracted.

In the cafés of Italy, the theatre of the operation and espresso method, occurs before the customer. This begins by removing the filter holder from the machine, left there together with the previous serving's spent coffee, in order to retain the heat in both, the machine and filter. Then, 'banging' out the remains into a waste-draw, beside or beneath the machine, the filter holder is offered up to the coffee grinder's dispenser, where a precisely measured and ground portion of coffee is collected, then pressed down via a tamping device. With the filter holder locked into the machine once more and upon a push of a button, or a pull from a sprung handle, a deep hum, a hiss and a gurgle, the espresso would be made. Although the system was primarily developed in and for the cafés, eventually sufficient demand was bound to have been created, for the initiated as well as long-standing devotees, to desire the taste and ceremony in their home.

Despite many advances in home espresso machines, however, the duplication of café quality espresso and cappuccino, especially using some of the cheaper appliances, remains a remote goal. Most of these conventional, inexpensive domestic appliances, sold for the purpose, cannot provide sufficient water and steam pressure to accomplish a good quality

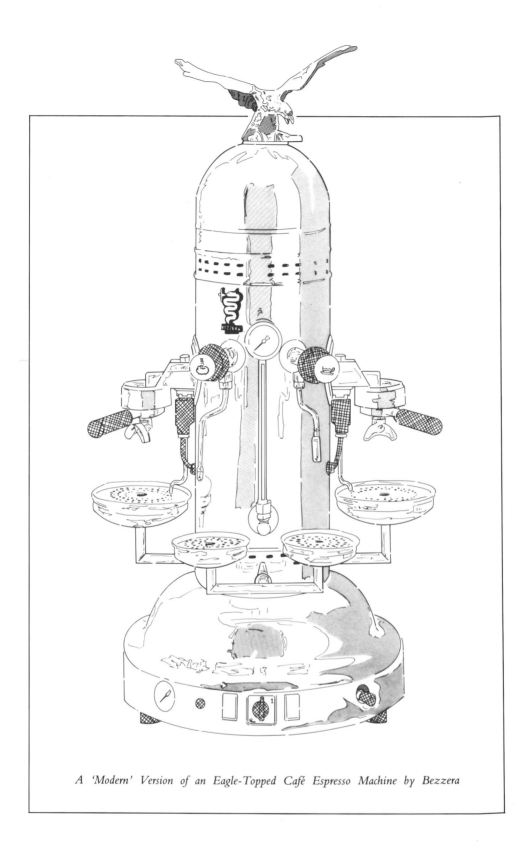

A 'Modern' Version of an Eagle-Topped Café Espresso Machine by Bezzera

cup of espresso, and literally run out of steam at the first frothing of milk for a cappuccino. Such systems do little for the promotion of authentic espresso and merely perpetuate misinterpretation of what after all, amongst connoisseurs would be regarded as the 'champagne method' of coffee brewing. At this point it is also worth mentioning, and particularly discouraging to find, that in view of a world-wide renaissance of the drink, with yet greater recognition of and demand for genuine espresso, the coffee world should witness the introduction of 'instant espresso' and 'instant cappuccino' to supermarket shelves. These products, should you be unfamiliar with their availability, rest assured, have nothing whatsoever in common with real espresso or cappuccino, not in taste, presentation, style and most importantly cannot be used in conjunction with your espresso maker. Because of their claim to producing espresso or cappuccino, when essentially these may only be accomplished with the proper method of brewing or rather infusion of the drink, these products should be viewed as a misrepresentation. For the purpose of this text, however, authentic espresso and how best to recreate the drink and it's cuisine at home, shall remain the only concern.

To achieve this and maintain with some consistency, will to a certain degree depend upon the quality as well as the type of machine or device used.

The earlier style café machines, the basic design of which may still be encountered today, were operated with a spring-powered piston via an external lever. Pulling the lever downwards, opened a valve inside, allowing a measured amount of water to be forced through the coffee. The spring would then return the lever slowly to it's upright position. The *Europiccola* by *La Pavoni* is such an example. Reminiscent of those shiny, eagle-topped towers, found in cafés throughout the thirties and forties, the Europiccola, chrome-plated or brass-finished, and table-top size, will certainly cause a mild sensation at most dinner parties. Rather than using the spring compression method of the café machines, the Europiccola uses a hand-powered piston to increase the steam pressure, held in the top of the water-tank, with the lever acting as the main force for pushing the water through the coffee. Controlled by a separate valve, the attachment for heating and frothing the milk protrudes from the side of the casing.

Enabling simpler and faster operation with a greater consistency of results, describe the characteristics of the 'new' style of machines, which substitute the spring powered piston with a hydraulic pressure system, enabling easier control, greater pressure build-up and various degrees of automation, literally at the touch of a button. Many catering establishments now take advantage of larger and yet more automated systems, incorporating electronically controlled, internal functions, for temperature, pressure and faster regeneration of both heat and steam, thereby satisfying even the busiest of demand for espresso and cappuccino.

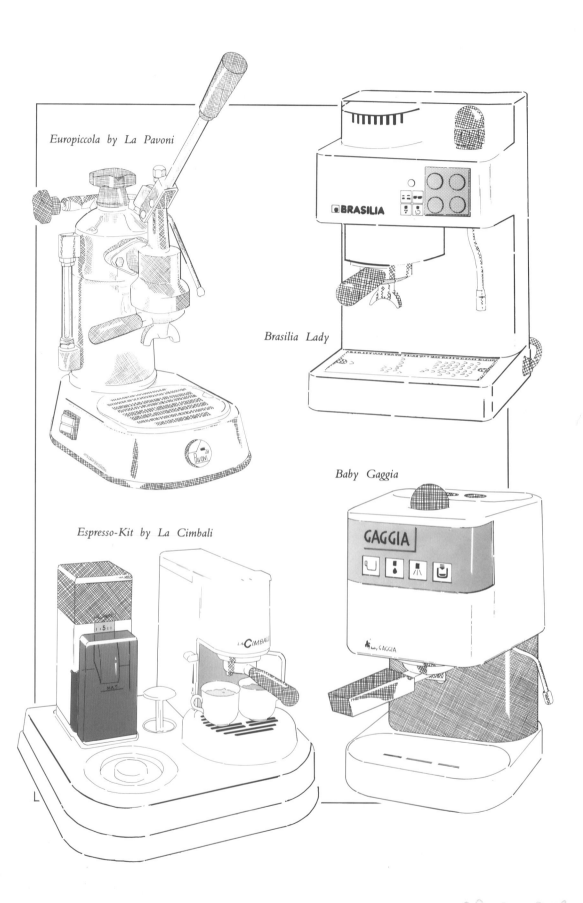

Europiccola by La Pavoni

BRASILIA

Brasilia Lady

Baby Gaggia

GAGGIA

Espresso-Kit by La Cimbali

Having recognised the burgeoning trend for domestic espresso cuisine, some of the manufacturers of professional equipment, have developed scaled down versions for home use, retail customer courtesy, office or the '20 cups-a-day' café. The *Baby Gaggia* could be considered one such development. Styled for the modern home, and the flagship of a range of domestic machines by *Gaggia*, it benefits extensively from the company's long-standing experience of manufacturing for the catering industry. *Brasilia* represents another Italian manufacturer, with deep-rooted traditions in the development and innovation of café espresso machines. Revered for exceptional build quality, service and design, Brasilia's examples for the home also reflect the efficiency, attributable to their catering units. Their *Club* and the recently introduced *Lady* machine with steam boost, combine push button convenience and the boxy looks of the modern café machines. Professional quality for the home.

(Recreating the recipes for the photographic illustrations of this book, required not only authentic espresso and cappuccino capability from a machine, but also for the authentic look to survive, without trickery, the complex and lengthy lighting procedures involved on the sets. The Brasilia 'Lady', which we choose to fulfil the task, proved more than adequate.)

Whilst the Europiccola and Baby Gaggia are available from specialist retail outlets, the Brasilia units are obtainable from the U.K. importers direct. (Please refer to our source guide for further information.) Priced similarly, these machines, at around £300, are likely to be aspired only by the ardent few of espresso devotees, intent on coupling café method with convenience, at any cost.

If you happen to fit into this category and you require yet greater choice, before finally deciding on a purchase, you will generally find it difficult to track down other professional quality, domestic systems, imported into the U.K. because the British distributors of such equipment, seem to maintain a low profile in promoting their products to the consumer.

However, one recently imported system, which we encountered during our research for this book, certainly merits mentioning. The *Espresso Kit* by *La Cimbali* at just over £330 provides very good value. It combines the *Cimbalina* machine and the *Uno* coffee grinder on a base unit. A practical and efficient, domestic solution to the preparation of café quality espresso and cappuccino. The above items may also be purchased separately. La Cimbali offer several units for home-use, with the dearest model, the *Domus Dosatron* costing over £500 but featuring a level of sophistication, usually found only on the larger café machines.

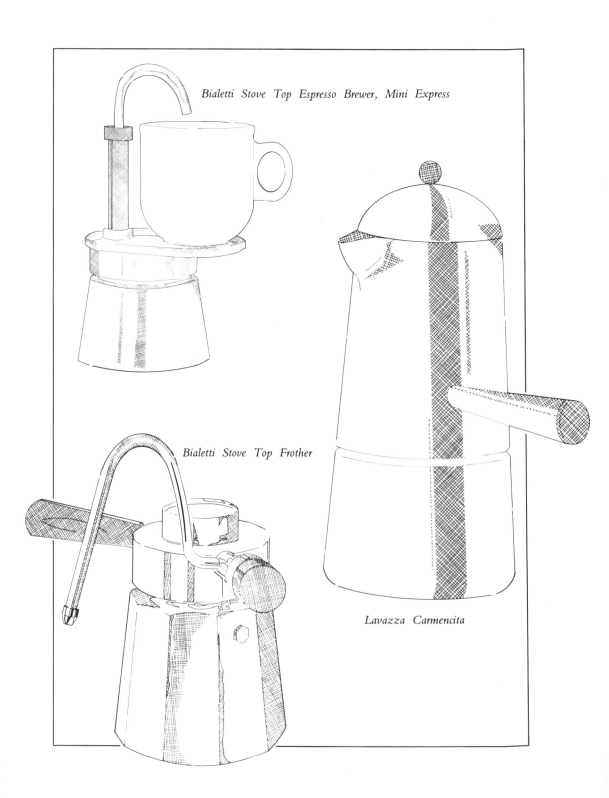

Bialetti Stove Top Espresso Brewer, Mini Express

Bialetti Stove Top Frother

Lavazza Carmencita

For those of you, wishing to replicate the taste with a lesser commitment of budget, although, strictly speaking not regarded as a true caffè espresso method, the stove-top espresso pots or brewers offer a good and low cost alternative, nevertheless able to provide a satisfactory espresso flavour when used correctly. From a one-cup to an eighteen-cup version, from the simple and well known *Moka Express* to the luxuriously finished *Carmencita* by *Lavazza*, they work on the principle of heating the water in a base-reservoir via external means such as your cooker-hob or stove-top. Once sufficient steam pressure has been generated in the reservoir, hot water is then forced upwards through a coffee-filled strainer into an upper receptacle for subsequent and prompt pouring into cups. You will need to experiment a little in order to achieve a consistently good cup of espresso. The right amount of ground coffee, grind quality, tamping pressure and duration of heat applied to the water, will vary with each different design of stove-top brewer.

Apart from cup-quantity and design, the choice of pot should also be based upon the materials used in manufacture. The cheaper versions, although adequate, are usually made from aluminium, which can taint the drink with a slightly metallic flavour. An additional drawback, particularly important with making espresso, is that aluminium conducts heat super-efficiently and therefore may cause the freshly brewed coffee in the upper receptacle to overheat and burn, ruining the delicate flavour of the espresso completely.

Some manufacturers overcome this problem by using stainless steel, others incorporate ceramic or porcelain receptacles. *Bialetti's* development of the pot, evolved the *Mini Expres*. With several cup versions available, it eliminates the need for collecting the coffee in a receptacle, by allowing the brewed coffee to dispense from a curved spout, straight into the cup. The integral platform also serves to pre-warm the cup. If cappuccino is your drink, there are now separate stove-pots for frothing the milk. With little difference in price, both, the *Graziella* version and Bialetti's seem to be the most popular. Made from aluminium, they retail at just over £20 and will provide sufficient steam pressure to enable a lasting cappuccino topping. For an all-in-one stove-pot, combining espresso brewing and milk frothing capabilities, the *San Remo* will also be appreciated for its stainless steel finish, at just under £40.

With a world of difference between the espresso experienced in Italy's bars, and that served elsewhere, a few exceptions apart, it has become difficult to accept just how much of the success for authentic caffè espresso is finally due to whatever machine, no matter how sophisticatingly simple, or whether after all, it is entirely owing to the passionate skills of the operator, the bar man or restaurateur, using whatever facilities with epicurean care. True of many places outside of Italy, few personnel operating café machines, know or care how to fulfil the requirement for espresso cuisine. From general misuse of machinery, to using the wrong coffee, as well as the seemingly universal inability to froth the milk for a cappuccino and the most common mistake in making espresso, the brewing of too much coffee from the grounds, resulting in a thin and bitter tasting concoction, should leave at least those interested in the concept, wondering at the worth of all that equipment and fuss and anyone else eager for what they know to be espresso, questioning whether to pay the bill.

Several recent visits to a London restaurant revealed, that in spite of a grinder with a hopper filled with coffee beans, annexed to the big machine, the proprietor preferred to make his espresso with ready ground coffee, scooped from a bulk-catering pack, thereby denying his custom that essential and ever-ready freshness, which makes espresso what it is. In a commercial establishment, serving espresso coffees, no grounds should be kept on hand for more than one hour. Another sample experience proved far more disappointing. Whilst conducting a business meeting in an hotel near London's Heathrow Airport, the promise of a good cup of espresso, judged upon sight of the machine behind the bar, turned out to be no better than a weak, black coffee, served with a tub-portion of half-cream, which had been balanced on the rim of the saucer.

All of which goes to show, that espresso needs to be made with love, or at least a passion, if not a sympathetic understanding of everything in contribution to the successful accomplishment of the drink, rather than leaving the entire process to whatever mechanical device. To grasp some of that passion, you certainly will need to have tasted a 'perfect' cup of coffee - at least once. A small, premier espresso is nothing less than the pinnacle of coffee drinking, one which will reward you with a burst of flavour, momentarily sensed throughout the mouth.

Several decades ago, real coffee was a luxury, reserved only for the most special of occasions and highly priced as an international commodity. Even today, its relatively high cost when compared to ordinary tea, occasionally prevents it from ending up in a supermarket-trolley, yet a cup of coffee costs less than an equivalent quantity of beer, wine or soft drink.

With little concern for those, who regard the drink as something hot and brown, to wake them up in the morning, the currently growing interest in coffee cuisine, and healthy trend away from the convenience-beverage by the same name, shows that for some, the discovery of the pleasure of genuine coffee is worth all the effort. Just as wine-lovers seek to marshall their taste-buds around the extraordinary, to the dedicated and connoisseurs of coffee, the drink presents an occasional but daily sensual delight, one respected and savoured with ceremonial deliberation, sometimes just to explore a different blend or method, sometimes to compliment a mood and often something to socialise over after a meal.

Espresso, worthy of much exploration and arguably the finest of coffee cuisines, not merely to the Southern European palate, but developing traditions globally, nevertheless as a method, shares in the same basic care and considerations, which benefit any other; – good water, (espresso machines in catering establishments are likely to be installed with a water-purification system), the quality of beans, blend and roast, the freshness of grind and careful brewing.

With regard to selecting the right whole-bean coffees from the varieties grown, much could be instructive, but to inform on all that is coffee, its history, traditions, geographical habitats and agricultural or roasting methods would indeed require ten times and more the pages available to the publication and its confinement to espresso. Revealing a smidgen, pertinent, nonetheless will be sufficient in providing some understanding.

With two basic kinds of whole-bean coffees grown, the hardiest and most resistant to disease is the aptly named *Robusta*. Indigenous to Africa, it grows at sea-level, on trees rather than bushes. Notwithstanding its inferior fragrance and flavour, robusta has become of major importance, as a blend-ingredient and for producing some of the cheaper instants. *Arabica*, or 'high-grown mild' which also includes the *Brazilian* category of coffees, in sharp contrast to the robustas, command the highest prices on the world markets. Cropped from bushes, which only flourish in certain well-watered regions of the tropics, at altitudes above 2000 feet and usually between 4000 – 6000 feet, arabica coffees represent the main source for the roasters to produce quality and speciality coffees.

Most speciality coffee roasters supply a 100% arabica blend for the espresso market. The better blends will probably consist of several and the best Central American coffees with a good proportion of Costa Rican whole-beans. These will have been 'high roasted' to a dark brown, to result in a definite, bittersweet tang, with all the acidity tones gone. Other roasters combine the Central American with Indonesian coffees which, when properly brewed yield a most excellent, thick, and caramelly-sweet espresso with a highly fragrant aroma. The tangy *Guatemala Antigua*, or the exotic *Ethiopia Yergacheffe* will also make superb espresso.

To standardise on a particular roast colour for espresso would mean to deny the varied traditions and preferences of and for espresso, which naturally have evolved in so many different ways, across Europe and the Americas. Therefore, you may come across a lightish dark brown roast, bitter-sweet chocolate brown in colour, in the US for example, whilst an Italian roast will be darker, with a French roast, the darkest and nearly black. But in each case the blend will have been carefully composed with different types of beans, whose flavours would be best suited to a particular roast. Also, for some afficionados, adding a small percentage of robusta beans to the predominant arabica blend, will improve the

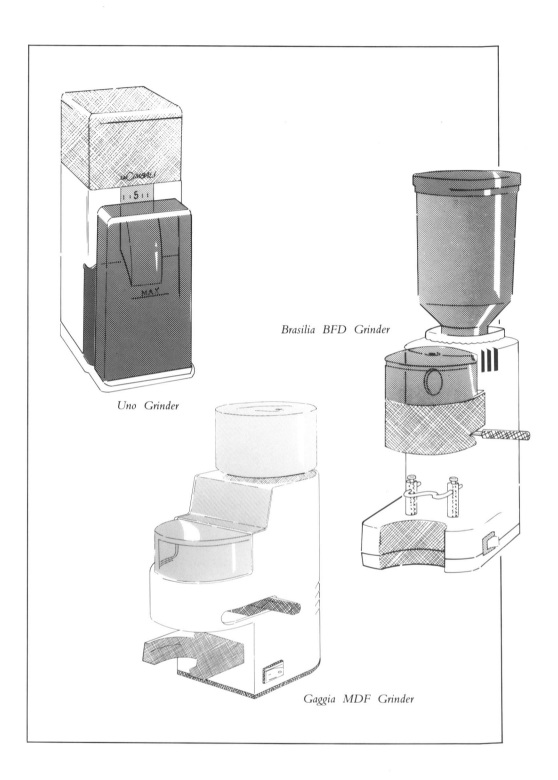

Uno Grinder

Brasilia BFD Grinder

Gaggia MDF Grinder

espresso's flavour by supplementing a marginal amount of acidity, lacking with the high-roasted arabica beans. It is said that this will give the espresso some 'snap' and 'brightness' as well as enhance its cup-presentation, by gaining an easier achieved crème, that 'bubbly', light-brown froth which indicates the proper brewing of espresso, possibly even compensating for any lack-lustre mode of operation. However, add too much of the robusta and its effervescent quality will make the crème just fizzle away before you get to drink the espresso. At this point, it might be pertinent to note that in view of the much varied and often poor quality of espresso, commercially served, the wrong choice of coffee and blend used, will commonly be to blame. After all which catering establishment wouldn't be tempted to increase their profitability by slipping in a few cheap beans now and then. It might also be pertinent to point out that just as much as we have come to expect a range of different ales across the bar, or have become accustomed to an enormous choice of wines, offered us in a good restaurant, will coffees, different blends, brewing methods and choice of flavourings ever be granted menu-status, upon sufficient demand?

Because green coffee maintains its freshness for years and some even improve with age, with only subtle changes to flavour, the best solution to drinking coffee as fresh as ever possible, would be the Arab way; roast, grind, brew and savour the drink, all in one, and accomplished in a half-hour sitting. Due to the Western approach to life and its perpetual requirement for convenience, we would assume that roasting your own, might prove a little impractical, if not unnecessary, in view of the availability of roasted coffees. Stored in a dry and airtight container, such as the hopper on a commercial grinder, roasted whole-beans should last for about a week, without losing much of the flavour and aroma. Preserving ground coffee is a different matter and quite futile. Once the ground coffee has been exposed to the air, the deterioration process begins and after a few hours, the coffee will start to go stale. The delicate oils evaporate quickly once exposed and although an airtight container will help, this will merely delay the deterioration. Therefore the best way to ensuring freshness will be to grind your own, although, the hand-grinding mills, 'quickie electrics' and general domestic grinders cannot provide the fineness, essential to making espresso, especially when high-pressure commercial quality units are used. Whereas the coffee for your cafetiere requires only a gauge 9 for its grind, espresso generally will need an almost icing sugar fineness, yet still feel gritty to touch, which a gauge 3 setting of grind will accomplish.

For espresso makers, working on a lower pressure of coffee infusion, the *Melitta*-style of grind will be sufficient and may be achieved by an inexpensive blade-grinder. Both, Gaggia and La Pavoni market suitable units for this type of application and for just under £20. Should you require a slightly finer, more powdery grind because you are using a high-pressure machine, you will need a burr-type coffee grinder. These represent quite

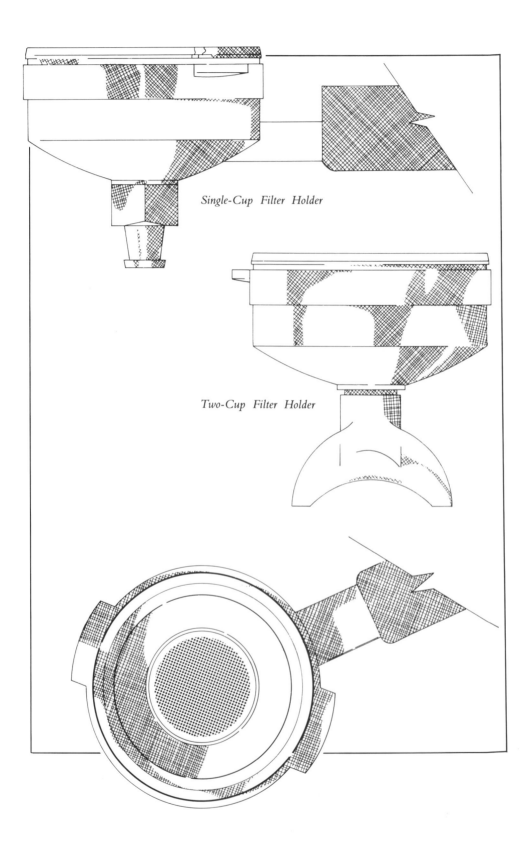

Single-Cup Filter Holder

Two-Cup Filter Holder

an expense, even with the cheapest model imported into the UK, the *Siemens KM70* which retails at just over £40. *Saeco* offer a unit at marginally over £70, the previously mentioned 'Uno' by La Cimbali £105, Gaggia's top-model, the *MDF* grinder, costs around £130 and Brasilia's *BFD* amounts to £195. These feature various settings for grind-fineness as well as a dosage-device for dispensing 6-7 grammes per espresso portion.

Anyone obsessed with drinking espresso at home, using a professional quality machine and intent on as fresh a coffee as is practically possible, which of course is what the drink is all about, will have to dig even deeper into their pockets, just to grind the beans to the correct fineness. If on the other hand, you cannot justify the expense, especially when this has to occur in conjunction with the purchase of a good quality espresso/cappuccino maker, you will need to buy your coffee ready ground and in small quantities. Should you be fortunate enough to live close to a specialist coffee-shop and happen to provide them with regular custom, you might be able to persuade them to grind you just 100g of your favourite espresso blend, which for a household of two persons represents about four days' worth. If however, you have to depend on the smallest, pre-packaged ready ground coffee, which is about 250g or around ten days of supply for the same household, you will have to sacrifice most of the freshness half way through that period, no matter how efficiently it is stored.

In this situation, probably the best method of storage, would be a small kilner-jar or any small glass-jar with a screw-top lid and a rubber gasket for additional sealing, in which to place the pre-ground coffee and then keeping the whole in your refrigerator. Although and inevitably comprising some of the freshness, essential to espresso, you will be able to keep a few days supply without too much loss of flavour and aroma.

If any of the aforementioned hasn't sent you back to the percolator, the next steps to making an espresso, will largely depend upon whether you are using the stove-pot method of brewing or a good quality domestic espresso/cappuccino maker. Assuming that you have ground your coffee fine enough, or you've obtained the right pre-ground blend and know your machine as per the makers instructions, the following procedure should be the same for most espresso/cappuccino machines.

With the unit warmed up, which depending on the model-design can take between 3 - 10 minutes, and may be indicated by the steam-button light going out or by some other means of ready-light, first run some water through the filter for a few seconds by activating the coffee brewing button. This will warm up the filter. Then unlock the filter holder (usually right to left), from the group-head of the machine and dispense of any residual water. If you are using pre-ground coffee or a grinder without a dosage-device, you will need to use the measuring spoon, normally provided with your machine, to scoop

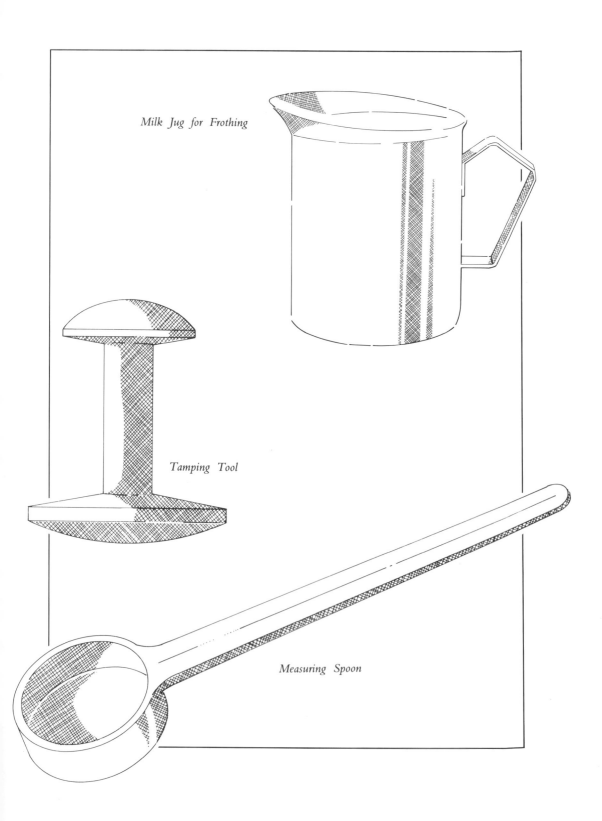

Milk Jug for Frothing

Tamping Tool

Measuring Spoon

a levelled amount of coffee which represents about 6 - 7 grammes, into the filter holder. If this is a two-cup filter, double the portion. Before returning the filter to the machine, press down the coffee evenly and firmly with the tamping device, supplied and designed to fit your type of filter. If your espresso flows too slowly, try a lighter tamp pressure. With the filter locked into the machine, press the brew button. You will notice immediately that the initial flow is quite dark, rich and syrupy, followed by a gradual thinning to a very light, frothy brown. This is because the best of the espresso comes out first, as the hot water efficiently removes all the flavoursome elements from the grounds, leaving almost nothing but the harsh and bitter traces for last. Therefore you will need to stop the brewing process at the right moment.

Generally, once your small espresso cup is about half full and some of the light, frothy brown flow has settled as the crème on top, your espresso or two will be made. Regarding the rate of pour for espresso, this may be likened to that of honey dripping from a spoon, to quote an ideal of description or a slow motion analogy. By experimenting with the grind, the dosage and tamping pressure, you can establish the best flow rate and the best flavour. Ideally, a single shot of espresso should result in $1 - 1\frac{1}{4}$ fluid ounces passing through the filter in about 20 seconds. With a two-cup filter and double the amount of coffee, the rate of pour should be accomplished in the same time as that for one portion.

Before you offer any of your guests a cappuccino, you might want to have a few practise runs first, although half way there, with the preparation of the coffee being the same as for espresso but for a different cup. Having the espresso occupying about a third of the cappuccino-cup, half fill a stainless steel jug with cold fresh milk. The shape of the jug is important. Avoid jugs with a spout or inverted rims, as the former will dispense more of the unfrothed milk and the latter prevent you from distributing the milk and froth, smoothly and evenly. Next, lower the steam-arm or pipe into the jug as far as possible without the nozzle actually touching the base. Press the steam-button and open the steam-valve fully and as quickly as possible. After a few seconds, lower the jug so that the nozzle is just below the surface of the milk, which will continue the aeration and heating procedure. As the milk begins to rise, nearly to the top of the jug, lower the steam-pressure by turning the valve in the opposite direction. This will be accompanied by a loud growling noise, as the milk begins to thicken. As a general rule of thumb, you should be able to determine the ideal temperature of the milk by feeling the outside of the jug which should be very warm and not too hot to touch. With sufficient froth, lay the milk onto the coffee by gradually tilting the jug, and with a rocking motion distribute equal amounts of milk and froth until almost level with the rim of the cup. You will notice that some of the coffee has coloured the edges of the froth.

The sequence for frothing the milk.

Step 1 Lower nozzle into the jug, without touching the base, then open steam valve.

Step 2 After approximately five seconds bring nozzle to just below the milk surface.

Step 3 As the milk begins to froth, slowly reduce the steam pressure to an audible growl.

A good cappuccino should consist of approximately ¹/₃ of espresso, ¹/₃ of hot steamed milk and ¹/₃ of foamed milk. You can garnish the top of the froth to suit your taste, or the time of day. In Italy, regarded as a breakfast drink, a cappuccino is rarely decorated. The sprinkling of the frothed milk with unsweetened cocoa, or cinnamon, grated bitter chocolate, or even instant-powder coffee, has developed from the middle European attitudes towards the drink, where it is preferred as an accompaniment to afternoon snacks or sweet pastries.

Once you've made your cappuccino, wipe off any residue milk left on the steam-arm, to prevent it from baking onto the metal. Always turn the steam valve on or off, while the arm is submerged in the milk, otherwise the force of steam will splatter the milk. The fresher and cooler the milk, the easier it will froth. Overheat the milk, or boil and you will have to start over because boiled milk cannot be frothed. Never use a porcelain or glass jug and ensure that the steel jug you choose for your machine is the right size. A ¹/₂ litre jug will be the maximum capacity practical for use with a domestic type of machine. While the machine is in use, clear the steam-arm of any condensed water, every so often and particularly before frothing, as well as afterwards in order to dispense of any trapped milk. Also run some water through the filter after the frothing is completed so that the next coffee delivery will be immediate. The filter holder should always be left attached to the machine, when in use, to maintain a working temperature, but removed when the machine is no longer required.

Because espresso is such a strong, sharply flavoured coffee, it is hardly the drink to consume in large quantities and certainly not a night-cap. With caffeine having sponsored much controversy and many fallacies, over the last three centuries, the minus side nevertheless exists. To find out, (not advisable), you would only need to drink several espressos in rapid succession, to feel the genuine toxic effects of nausea, chilliness and disorientation. Therefore, the only answer to the problem, as with many things in life, would seem to be one of simple moderation - maintaining coffee as an occasional tonic, not a toxin.

For anyone concerned with the long-term effects of caffeine on their health, yet still in love with espresso, you will find several decaffeinated versions such as the *Lavazza Dek*, available from your coffee-shop. These produce a good cup of espresso without the added stimulation of caffeine, which will allow you to enjoy any of the espresso/cappuccino variations described over the following pages, or adapt your own versions from the basic Italian coffee-cuisine such as these oft-encountered serving options.

Espresso

The basic, single demitasse of no more than two fluid ounces of black coffee, often drunk with sugar and may be flavoured with a range of extracts such as almond, orange or liqueur substitutes.

Espresso Ristretto

Meaning 'restricted' or 'narrow', it is a common variation of the basic espresso and is achieved, by shortening the pour to just one fluid ounce. Very strong.

Espresso Romano

A single espresso served with a curl of lemon peel or just a sliver of lemon on the side.

Espresso Macchiato

Macchiato means 'marked' or 'spotted' and this is what happens to a straight espresso, by 'marking' the top with a smidgen of foamed milk.

Espresso Con Panna

The same as above, except for serving the espresso with a tiny topping of whipped cream.

Espresso Mocha

This is usually served in a mug and is made up of one-third espresso, one-third of strong, unsweetened hot chocolate and one-third of frothed milk which goes in last.

Doppio

Simply a 'double' of straight espresso, best left to the veterans of espresso.

Cappuccino

Approximately one-third espresso, one-third hot, steamed milk and one-third frothed milk.

Caffè Latte

Usually one or two measures of espresso with three times as much foamed milk. Pour both milk and coffee simultaneously, from either side of the cup. An ideal breakfast-drink, if you can find the dexterity.

Latte Macchiato

A large tumbler half-filled with hot, foamed milk, into which a single espresso is slowly poured to produce a graduation of coffee-colour through the milk.

The many and varied traditions for enhancing coffee with other flavouring substances, to dilute or fortify the drink, is not at all unique to the espresso method. The espresso method simply brings them from promise to perfection.

esprit d´espresso

Part Two

Serving Suggestions
&
Espresso-Times-Of-The-Day

Coffee as much as the flavour of wine is experienced by its volatile qualities, those elements which we encounter with our sense of smell and taste. One of the reasons we find coffee interesting is because it is especially aromatic when compared to something like cream. Equally true of coffee, the warmer something is, the more fragrant it becomes. Take any cooking process, for instance or think of how much baking and roasting contribute to flavour and aroma.

Coffee to the purist is to drink it black - 'au nature' as the French put it. However in many parts of the world, the traditions for supplementing coffee with other flavours, has resulted in many a happy association.

For a delicate sensation on the palate, try flavouring your coffee with a strip of lemon peel, the Italian way, or sprinkle some grated orange and lemon peel onto the drink to excite your taste-buds. In Russia, inclined by old customs, the preference will extend to squeezing a little lemon juice into the coffee. While Ethiopians like to develop the finer flavours by adding a pinch of salt, the Moroccans will aim for maximum kick from their drink, by immersing whole black peppercorns.

And of course, many traditions exist for lacing coffees with spirits or liqueurs, whose own volatile elements simply flourish when merged with hot coffee, originating many sensational flavours and perfumes.

Espresso, generally, offers the best marriage with other flavours and is particularly well chosen for use with iced coffee recipies, when a stronger sort of coffee helps to stem the dilution of taste. Chase an espresso with a liqueur or a cognac and even the most jaded of palates will refresh. Add steamed or frothed milk to a base of espresso, and all the milky coffees in the world stand challenged by the richness of taste that culminates in cappuccino.

It is hoped that at least some of the delightful serving suggestions for espresso, described over-leaf, will ultimately contribute to your enjoyment of the drink, - and that sharing our personal encounters or anecdotally recounted 'espresso-times-of-the-day', which nevertheless originated the few 'recipes', be merely perceived as an occasional mood, or perhaps a special moment, long past, an individual's fortune recalled over the drink or as just one of those peculiarities of life, best taken the same way an Ethiopian prefers his coffee –

Whilst on a photographic excursion to Naples, and venturing into one of the local churches, I learnt that the Padre had just concluded a particularly tedious bout around the font, preparing bare souls for, what was hoped, a lifetime of devout Catholicism. This sort of work always tried the Padre's patience.

Upon introduction, I witnessed a hint of pleasance about his face, as he beckoned me to attend him in the vestry. With an agility, belying his quite rotund appearance, the Padre proceeded to prepare us, what he announced to be an appropriate antedote to any stressful occasion.

He had simply discovered, that by accompanying an espresso with a generous measure of Vin Santo or Holy Wine, peace would return to his brow once more. Dipping a few morsels of *Cantuccini* biscuits into the fortified wine would complete the heavenly combination.

To reserve *Padre's Relief* for special occasions would indeed mean to deny yourself.

Appropriate as an elevens, or presented at a dinner party, this espresso, sipped in turns with an accompaniment of *Vino Santo*, justly measured into a liqueur glass, into which a *Cantuccini* or two should be dipped to prolong the experience of both taste and ceremony, will add a fine touch to entertaining your guests as well as lift your spirits, when by yourself.

Vino Santo, a fortified wine from Tuscany, was traditionally used as an altar-wine in Italy's churches. In the U.K. it is obtainable from specialist off-licenses and vintners.

Padre's Relief

That year, on business in the South of France, I had made many an early start at a café not far from my lodgings in La Napoule. Penning a few messages to a friend and catching up with world news, whilst dunking a croissant in my coffee, I had been party to the same routine performed before me every morning.

For 'Tormentia', a name I had conjured to be aptly fitting, would surely soon return to Barcelona. Her arduous task, I had assumed, of being a film critic at Cannes, would be drawing to a close.

Her 'final' morning had brought her, as ever, to the same café. Upon entering, this peculiar ceremony would unfold, as it had on each previous occasion.

Pierre, le patron, shoe-horned into black hipsters and shod in patent leather, Cuban-heeled boots, would rush over to 'Tormentia', performing a kind of flamenco, to climax with an emphatic 'Olé'. Then, shuffling back, with arms folded, he'd regard 'Tormentia' with an inquiring air.

'Tormentia' adopting her usual, ambivalent attitude to Pierre's attentions, would gracefully remove her corsage and hesitate in contemplation. This moment would cause Pierre tremendous, palm-perspiring anxiety. He wasn't getting any younger. At last she would concede her order. "Une Café Olé, s'il vous plait."

'Tormentia' always began her day with a milky coffee.

For those, who prefer a gentle start to their day, *Café Olé* provides mellow encouragement.

Pour a single espresso into a large, bowl-shaped cup. Then heat three or four times the quantity of cold milk via the steam-arm, taking care not to froth the milk. Keeping the pressure-valve in the mid-way position and the arm close to the base of the jug will aerate the milk and bring it up to the necessary heat, without loosing it's creaminess. Add to the coffee and accompany with a croissant on the side for a continental style of awakening.

Café Olé

I had rubbed shoulders with this character at someone's graduation bash. The following, doubtlessly embroidered, had probably only been recounted to me because of my known and continued fascination for coffee cuisine.

Ted, a one time market-stall trader from Bethnal Green, had decided to give up the hard graft, change his name to Eduardo and become a gigolo, frequenting towns along the Riviera.

Despite having tempered his East London origin and adopting only a mildly broken Italian accent, Eduardo would occasionally lapse into his old ways, especially after an excess of wine. This quite naturally would evoke looks of consternation from his bejewelled ladies, as he could be heard, calling,

"Signior, anuvva bo'el of She-anti, preygo."

Another of his questionable habits involved warming a miniature of *Amaretto* at the restaurant table, using matches or a candle. Pouring the warmed liqueur into his and his partner's espresso, would result in a delightful concoction, upon which he would inevitably be forgiven.

Eduardo had always been puzzled why his counterparts were rewarded with Alfas and Ferraris, when in his five years as a male escort, he'd only ever aspired to the gift of a Fiat 500.

For those, who enjoy a wonderfully aromatic tipple,
Gigolo's Pardon will charm any after-dinner ritual.

In an espresso-cup warm a measure of *Amaretto* by using
the steam-arm of your machine. This will enhance the
liqueur's rich, almond fragrance. Top with a standard
quantity of espresso, and have the crème conceal the
sensation beneath. The *Amaretto* will make adding sugar
unnecessary, except perhaps for the sweetest of palates. To
complete the indulgence, unashamedly dunk a few
Cantuccini biscuits to soak up the mingling of flavours.

Gigolo's Pardon

"Consider the agony aunt", my sociology lecturer had orated. Well yes, I had considered agony aunts on many occasions, not out of necessity for having to correspond but quite simply because my mother's sister happens to be one.

A curious profession, I thought, for someone who confessed, although not publicly, to the life of a happily confirmed spinster. I had therefore always marvelled at her prowess in providing others with profound marital advice. However on the eve of her fortieth birthday, I was to experience her secret.

I had wanted to give her my present before she left for the opera. When I arrived, she had just prepared a 'sharpener', an espresso topping a shot of *Baileys*, however the ring of the telephone summoned her to an adjacent room. With a sudden and overwhelming urge to satisfy my curiosity, I had begun to search the closely guarded contents of her handbag.

Upon opening my eyes, seeing my aunt bent over me, red faced and smelling salts in hand, I realised, that I was still clutching the two wedding photographs, which had borne witness to not only one but two failed marriages.

Oh, the agony of my aunt.

Moments savoured with *Café Solo Con Baileys* turn special affairs into simple pleasures.

Pour a generous measure of *Baileys* into an espresso-cup, leaving adequate room for a single espresso on top. The creamy combination of three different flavours will pamper even the most peevish of tastes.

Café Solo con Baileys

Navigating our sloop, L'Espiegle, chartered out of St. Nazaire, into Dieppe for an urgent repair to a leaky bilge, eventually found me in this port-side bar, where I was cheerfully rewarded with this well worn tale about a latter day Channel Island rogue.

Apparently in the mould of Long John Silver, there followed a somewhat less famous, but equally infamous contender, who assumed the name of Gaff Roy Gold, a one time Jewish merchant converted to less auspicious enterprises, preferring to run his 80ft ketch alongside many a pleasure vessel, 'Just for protection', comprenez vous.

Despite many years on the ocean waves, Gaff was still prone to severe sea-sickness, especially when caught in rough seas. The merest sniff of a storm would send him scurrying into port and into the nearest bar for comfort. One of his mercy dashes took him to the self same bar in the port of Dieppe, where he too discovered fishermen imbibing copious quantities of espresso and *Calvados* chasers, whilst competently tossing pistachio nuts into the air and catching them with jaws apart.

After initiating himself to this soothing combination, Gaff declared his gratitude by ordering a Café Calve for every customer in the bar.

I too felt dutibound.

After an early day's chore, rekindling one's spirits, or
kick-starting the day for outdoor leisure-activities,
Pirate's Urge, an espresso accompanied with a separate
measure of *Calvados*, will impose a distinctly European
tone on your palate. For a more relaxed version of
coffee-break, supplement the drink with a proportionate
helping of pistachio nuts.

Pirate's Urge

Cooey had no inhibitions presuming herself a present day Marilyn Monroe. Her wannabe demeanour was absolute, from her peroxide blonde hair to her sartorial deportment.

Her talents for being cast on the couch were an esteemed pursuit for some, and a source of curiosity for others, both landing her with the same outcome.

A recent morning had found her waking with the haze of the night's excesses, somewhere in the palatial estate of Felix Bogusso, a Spanish film director. Felix, concerned for Cooey's fragile looks promptly instructed remedial breakfast, a dip in the pool followed by a frothy orange flavoured cappuccino. Cooey's perkiness, thus returned, could have made many an eye sparkle.

"Oh Felix", she exclaimed, "What would I do without you?"

Felix's eyes narrowed.

To prepare this Cappuccino, stir approximately 18-20
drops of orange-flavouring into the coffee, before you add
the frothed milk, then finish with a sprinkling of
cocoa powder.

The subtle tanginess of orange, not sharp but delicate, will
enhance your breakfast of marmalade and toast.

Orange Splash

I had heard much about this entrepreneurial spirit, however meeting him was to prove a less endearing experience.

The founder and self-ordained leader of the Right Righteous Evangelical Church, the Right Reverend Jim Storm, was a particularly controversial soul. He had shunned traditional, religious apparel in favour of sharp Italian suits. To Jim, theological matters were a means to an end, and that did not necessarily mean a one way ticket to heaven. Decreed as fact finding missions, with which he could temper his sermons, his dubious pursuits would also provide him with the opportunity to be amongst those who most needed him. However his hands-on approach especially where contentious issues were concerned, had often landed him in trouble. His recent preachings on adultery being just one such example.

In preparation for an intended sermon on the perils of gambling, Jim chose to visit a backroom 'casino' near the Mexican border, to avail himself of the appropriate inspiration at one of the poker tables.

As the evening progressed, Jim had kept his mind alert by drinking large cappuccinos, the milk discreetly laced with *Batida*, a South American coconut liqueur, ensuring an outward aspect of relevant sobriety.

That night God was on Jim's side and he emerged the fortunate victor. With a smug twitch and gleeful regard he pronounced to me: "The Lord giveth and The Lord taketh away."

Café Batida de Coco is a cappuccino surprise and at first glance not much different to any other frothy milk-topped espresso, until you taste the rich coffee through the most sumptuous layer of coconut froth – a thoroughly relishable experience.

To prepare, first pour the coffee into a cappuccino cup. Then, combining approximately two parts of milk and one part of *Batida*, or a similar coconut liqueur, froth the mixture as normal and spread over the coffee. Additional sweetening is not advised.

Café Batida de Coco

A few months ago, browsing through some old magazines in the loft, I came across a lengthy account, made to the Old Bailey in 1934, by a companion witness to the accused; condensed here for brevity.

Society's reaction to the death of Lord Hamilton had not been particularly sympathetic. Even the dismissal of the entire kitchen staff by his widow, following the fatal food poisoning incident, had failed to sway public opinion.

The Countess regarded her newly acquired freedom of wealth as carte blanche, especially where her indulgence in haute couture and world travel were concerned. As one journal had declared, "Lady Rubinia's appetite for expanding her wardrobe, is commensurate only to her desire for wealthy, young men."

This sort of press eventually began to consume her benevolence, and priorities demanded a suitable distraction. Therefore, a voyage to New England, in order to oblige a long standing admirer, would more than adequately fulfil her needs.

On board one evening, soon after departure, and upon retiring from the ship's lavish entertainment, the Countessa had found herself at one of the tables on the upper deck. With a deep sigh, she registered her emptiness. Witnessing the jaded scenario, a bright, young lieutenant promptly offered his chocolate cappuccino, which would soon return her good spirits. Lady Rubinia's arms reached for the lieutenant, she was frightfully grateful.

Warmth, pleasure and soothing conjured from a
single cup.

This cappuccino is ordinary only as much as the coffee.
Instead of milk, add a topping of frothed cocoa. The
slightly, bitter edge, ideally, should remain by not over-
sweetening the drink. Garnish with a light dusting of
unsweetened cocoa-powder.

Countessa de Cocoa

One is never far from a story in a barber's shop. This one had probably sustained two generations of apprentices.

After years of eroding the truth, my own version seems just as likely.

Luca, the son of an American-Italian oil baron, was thrilled at finding accommodation so soon. The owner, a Ms. Rosamonde Critchley-Smythe appeared helpful and his new life in London was looking fortuitous.

Six months advance rental however made him feel a little encumbered, but as Ms. Critchley-Smythe was quick to clarify, such security for a well-appointed abode was the customary procedure. Eventually convinced, he settled the amount and was rewarded with the key.

The following day, he transferred his belongings and soon began to fit in. By lunchtime he was ready for a Great British take-away to be followed by a cappuccino laced with Crème de Cacao, one of his father's old tricks.

An unexpected knock on the door, however, interrupted the meal and was about to change Luca's sense of well being, for standing before him were two officers from Scotland Yard. Their abrupt request for an explanation as to his presence in the home of a Mr. Rupert Hanbury, currently in Europe, left him pale. Not a word, Luca thought, of "hello, hello, hello."

This certainly wasn't the movies.

Caffè Crème de Cacao is a perfect 'after food' cappuccino.
Any meal, no matter how basic, will assume an air of
'bon vivant', when completed with this drink.

Pour a single measure of *Crème de Cacao* into the cup,
add the coffee and frothed milk and garnish with a little
grated, dark continental chocolate.

Caffè Crème de Cacao

Attending a social worker's convention in the bible belt on Boxing Day one year, as the final preparation to an intended thesis for my sociology doctorate, landed me with this theatrical account.

From the general store window, the crocodile evening bag had beckoned relentlessly. With the Louisiana Cotton Pickers Ball only a month away, the desire to possess the stylish accessory had driven Mary-Lou to desperation. The $450 bag would look stunning next to her hand-me-down, star spangled ball gown.

However, many years of supporting her younger twin sisters, a terminally unemployed father and an alcoholic mother, who only last fall had absconded with the owner of a rum distillery, had left Mary-Lou miserably off, if not out of touch with life in general. Thus the plan to trap a crocodile and make her own bag had been hatched.

Invigorated by many glasses of a rum-laced coffee, a legacy from her mother's adulterous escapades, she finally had made her way to the jetty.

According to the confessions of John-Boy Waine, the last person ever to have seen Mary-Lou alive, she had slipped into the moonlit Mississippi never to return.

John-Boy is currently serving a second term in jail for gross voyeurism.

For this drink, pour a sweetened espresso into a tall, ice-charged tumbler. Swirl to chill and add a shot of dark Jamaican rum. Top with a little cold milk, stir and refresh with memories of summer-beaches and moon-lit coves. For adventurous tastes, or to extend the ceremony of preparation, you could sweeten the espresso by squeezing the sap out of a stick of sugar-cane.

Moonshine

Stim Blompson, now a freelance historian, who years ago had co-lectured with me on several occasions, had then specialised in the provenience of Icelandic culture. He had spent endless hours chipping at various rock sites in an attempt to prove that this nation had once been one of the most cultured and advanced civilisations in existence. He'd always believed their demeanour to have exceeded that of the Egyptians.

One of his climbs to an unyielding volcano summit had almost proved fatal. On reaching the col before the final ascent, Stim had collapsed, physically exhausted and despite the icy conditions had suffered a marked increase in body temperature.

Whilst recovering from his frailness, he had noticed a craggy glow emanating from a fissure, releasing a concentration of heat.

Even on successive climbs he would always make his way towards the spot, armed with his old faithful espresso maker and prepare himself a revitalising iced coffee. The icy fix of caffeine would provide Stim with a youth-like step as he'd continue to the summit.

For simple thirst-quenching, or keeping a cool head,
Café con Hielo provides a quick recipe.

On a small tray place a freshly brewed espresso, some
sugar and a small to medium-sized tumbler, crammed with
ice. Melt the sugar, to taste, in the espresso, pour into
the glass and complete the performance by swirling the
whole until chilled.

Café con Hielo

Maria, saddened after parting with Mario, her lover of three years, and just before my innocent encounter with her, at a veterinary clinic in Sao Paulo, had decided to steal herself off to a remote Caribbean island.

Flushed with a renewed sense of purpose, Maria had spent a glorious 14 days taking in the sun and a cooling, iced coffee and rum mixture from the beach bar.

On her last day, as the sun was melting the horizon, Maria's gaze beheld a dejected looking figure at the waters edge, ruefully strumming a guitar.

Despite his sagging shoulders and bowed head, she recognised him as the once beloved cat of the blues, Papa Mo Johnson. With tender curiosity Maria eased over to Papa Mo. Relaxing his poise to acknowledge the intrusion, a slight smile returned to bolster his sunken cheeks.

Only after he struck the opening chords of "Ain't got no pants blues," did Maria grasp her natural disposition, as her face merged with the setting sun.

Whenever the taste of tropical islands – without airport-delays – takes your fancy, this deliciously cool drink will make ideal transportation.

Into a cocktail-shaker place three to four ice-cubes, add one espresso, sweetened to taste, one shot of white rum with an equal measure of *Malibu* and approximately 200ml of chilled, fresh milk. Ceremoniously shake for about 20 seconds, and discharge the contents into a tall tumbler, filled with ice – for maximum chilling. Definitely for muggy days.

Café au Naturelle

Anbangbang, an aboriginal, tribal elder had always been found in a fit of frantic activity leading up to the 20th of January or thereabouts, which in his half of the hemisphere signified the longest day of the year.

As an annual treat to his band, as well as a token of thanksgiving, he had always prepared a refreshing *Eggagonggong*, to herald the dawning of the day. In Anbangbang's part of the world however, making the drink posed many problems.

Trying to bribe truckies with tribal bark paintings, seemed an impossible task over which crucial days could be wasted. Eventually though, one such truckie would part with the precious ice and milk, leaving Anbangbang to source the first laid egg of a batch, in order to fulfil the subtle flavour of the drink.

The French missionary, who'd related the recipe to me at a Northern Territory sheep station, had referred to the refreshment as "Premier Cuvee."

Intriguingly, Aborigines actually lay claim to discovering the espresso method long before the Italians. Italian afficionados of the bean hotly dispute this and simply put it down to dreamtime.

Serves Two

Into a blender pour two sweetened espressos, one egg and approximately 300ml of cold milk. Whisk for about five seconds, or until a foamy head has formed. Then distribute the mixture into two ice-filled tumblers.

An ideal beverage between meals, light but substantial, *Eggagonggong* will pacify even minor pangs of hunger.

Eggagonggong

"Zum Engelchen" was a cellar bar close to the Mosel in the quaint town of Bernkastel Kues, when my great uncle first visited the place. Then the establishment was being run by Else Wachtmeister, an attractive woman, if somewhat introverted, in her early thirties.

As the possibility of war gained momentum, the Wehrmacht, aware of Fräulein Wachtmeister's casual acquaintance with a certain Major Tarquin Pendelton, invited her to secure any relevant information concerning the general British course of action.

Although she had a soft spot for the old boy, her commitment stayed firmly with the Fatherland, besides the Wehrmacht meant more frequent and profitable custom.

One night, a rather pensive Major entered the bar straight into the arms of Else. It required a significantly stiff upper lip, ignoring Else's uncharacteristically seductive advances, and to remain oblivious to the sensation from her heaving and barely concealed breasts.

After seemingly endless smalltalk, prattle about his prize winning dahlias and having to hear about the bottle stall he had been organising for his village fete, Else fled into the kitchen. She mixed herself a *Slivovitch* coffee topped with cream, giving her the chance to collect her thoughts and consider another approach.

Meanwhile, the Major, counting on such a moment, had carefully pinned the very latest listening device onto one of the ceiling beams. Returning with the coffee, Else noticed the Major readying himself to leave, bicycle clips in place and quipping about getting his beauty sleep.

Alone once more, nodding to her drink, Else sighed, "Englischer Dummkopf".

Pour a measure of *Slivovitch* into a cappuccino-size cup,
together with a tea-spoon of brown sugar and gently heat
using the steam-arm. Once the sugar has dissolved, prepare
a double serving of espresso and pour into the same cup.
Top with some lightly whipped British double-cream,
floated off the back of a spoon.

The sensation of tasting the rich, hot coffee through the
cool topping will bring a generous flourish to your
culinary entertainment.

Café Rumbo

The deeply rooted urge for leaving the grimy dankness of his railway arch lock-up in South London once and for all, had stimulated Arthur Dali into drastic action. Trading in contraband had lost it's romantic appeal. Freed from ignorance, his creative side had beckoned and following a crash course in modern art, and dubious finance, Arthur had opened his first gallery in London's Fulham Road. A second outlet followed soon after, providing him also with a penthouse suite above.

His chirpy Cockney persona had become a bit of a gimmick in the high-falutin circles of the art world, with many a buyer wrongly assuming the possibility of a bargain. Arthur had learnt all there was to learn and coupled with his street wise shrewdness, gave him the ultimate edge with any deal.

Never minding his nouveau success, Arthur did not entirely embrace a champagne lifestyle. Indeed his favourite drink, a coffee flavoured milk shake, first quaffed at Mario's, a cafe next to his old lock-up, had remained a partiality.

Serves Two

Pour two sweetened and chilled espressos into a blender,
add about 250ml of cold milk and three generous scoops
of Italian vanilla ice-cream, or any other good quality ice-
cream, whisk for approximately five seconds, or until
frothy, then decant into two medium-sized tumblers.

An irresistible milkshake, slightly reminiscent of one's
formative years, when days were care-free and life
mortgage-less.

Art's Choice

Soon after arriving at the Manhattan Prospect night club, one wintry evening, a sophisticated looking guy, who introduced himself as Roger, began to monopolise the conversation with Tracy. There wasn't any denying that Tracy had welcomed the intrusion.

Roger's revelations of being a bit of a talent scout for a London model agency as well as having a fondness for the odd exotic sports car, left her in little doubt, that luck was taking a better turn.

Tracy had always believed that a modelling career was meant for her.

An invite to his apartment, received the expected response.

Moments later, with arms around each other's waist, Tracy's steps were being directed assuredly towards Roger's car. Tracy froze, her glossed lips quivering with disbelief. Was it possible that after nine brandy and babychams, a Ferrari could assume the guise of an embellished Capri?

An hour later, soaked in a hot bath, Tracy's dreams became sweet once more, with a coffee, some brandy and a hot chocolate topping.

There are no pretentions with this drink.

Into an espresso-cup draught a shot of dark Jamaican rum,
add one tea-spoon of brown sugar and gently heat with
the steam-arm of your machine. Once the sugar has
dissolved, brew a ristretto and top the 50/50 mixture with
a light coating or flecking of frothed unsweetened cocoa,
i.e. by scooping just a little of the froth with a spoon to
dress the top of the drink.

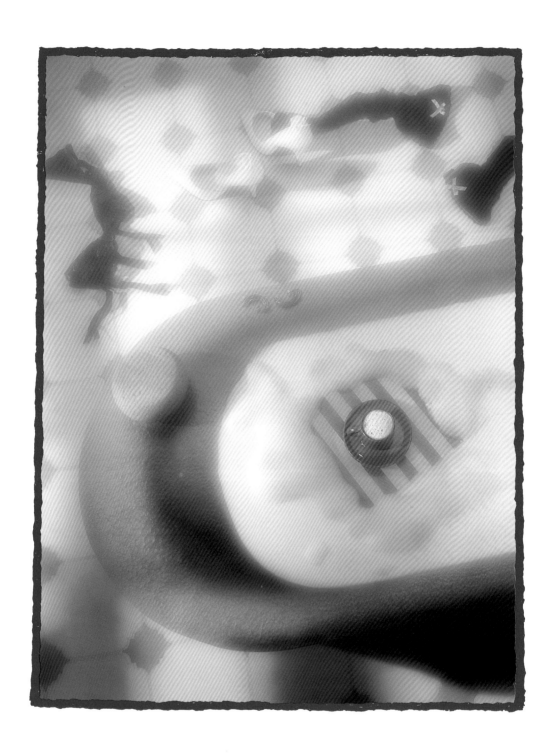

Manhattan Prospect

An unusual route into the world of haute couture. One could have been forgiven to scoff, but designing clothes for Barbie and her darling Ken, had actually stood Dutch designer, Nerp Van Drerp in good stead.

From a lofty warehouse apartment in Greenwich Village, Nerp had soon progressed to larger dummies. Most of the producers of popular soap operas had been keen enough to seek out the flamboyance of his style and flair for costumery. Thanks to Nerp, women sported their shoulders sharp. Anything up to 30" had become 'de rigeur'.

With the 80's gone, so ended Nerp's look. A change was a little overdue, and innovation not a weekly occurrence. However Nerp was ready. Several glasses of chilled coffee, cream, brandy and *Crème de Cacao* were to compound his future prospects.

The transition into the world of canine fashion was a thunderous success. In most well to do suburbs all over the States, dapper dogs could be seen cutting a dash, as they were being promenaded, nose and tail aloft.

No longer the drink for 'haute monde', an
American Dream, nevertheless achieves the aspirations,
expected of a 'racy' cocktail.

To a standard quantity of espresso add a jigger of cognac,
Crème de Cacao and a dollop of British double cream.
Transfer to a blender with a scoop-ful of ice-cubes, whisk
to a velvety texture and serve in a tall, slim glass.

American Dream

"Any job is better than none, especially in times like these", but Rhona wasn't so sure. The vacancy at the pottery, left by her mother, had given Rhona the opportunity of work, but applying mundane decorations to pieces of china, had never been her ambition.

Coping with Thimble, her floor manager was going to be another matter. He was hardly all things to all women. His snowflecked shoulders, the least of his shortcomings, probably had only ever felt the tears of disappointment, and yet his persistence in chasing after the ladies remained relentless.

Rhona, now part of his flock, had noted Thimble's initial attentions grow into lustful infatuation, so far however had managed to evade any advance with female cunning.

But dodging Thimble would only hasten his craftiness, and his eyes could be seen flickering with anxiety behind those milk-bottle-bottom glasses.

Just before the working day was done, he decided on a subtle approach, one which would not fail to engage Rhona's attention as well as pave the way for a proposal of dinner.

When Thimble's bid appeared on the conveyor, Rhona gasped, for in her colleagues absence, this was obviously meant for her. Sensing a presence she glanced over her shoulder to where Thimble was hovering, gleefully awaiting her response. "Why Mr Thimble, your zip's undone" Rhona replied.

Alone once more she reached for the chocolate mint liqueur, savouring each sip. Perhaps Thimble had a little charm after all.

Ideal for the rituals of 'dimanche cuisine', this drink will
round off the finest of Sunday roasts.

Pour a generous shot of mint chocolate liqueur into an
espresso-cup, add the espresso but discount the sugar.
Accompany with chocolate mint sticks.

Café Mint Choc

From his second floor apartment in La Bocca, a suburb of Buenos Aires, Fernandez would sit and lament his former glory days, for once he had been the most revered crooner in all Argentina.

With a string of hits, an even greater string of women and an ego as immense as the pampas, his fall from grace had been a difficult cross to bear.

The undignified end to his career had come unexpectedly. Catapulted from his favourite stallion on the eve of a major sell-out concert, the indelicate landing had not only left him teary-eyed, but had obscured his voice by several octaves.

One of his preprandial pleasures, he maintains to this day, apart from a former groupie, is a deliciously reviving coffee and brandy covered with chocolate milk.

After many of these drinks, the following morning would have his vocal cords a little deeper, but not for long.

Therefore Fernan' still ekes an existence providing voice-overs for Micky Mouse on local TV.

Fill your glass with ice, pour in a sweetened espresso and swirl to chill. Add a shot of brandy, ideally a Spanish one to accomplish a more mellow flavour, and top with chilled chocolate milk. The result - a cool drink for the 'laid back' time of a day, a 'snack' at any time or just before your empanadas, and certainly a delight for chocoholics.

Café Fatale

Educated at the Sorbonne and now in control of the family estate, Isabelle had not felt inclined towards the tedium of employment, in fact since the receipt of her inheritance, work in any form had become a phenomenon. Eventually though, many idle hours had amounted to a lot of boredom.

François came from the other side of the tracks and provided the diversion Isabelle had sought. She would, François mused, lend respectability to their crimes.

This particular evening had been coordinated for a late rendezvous in a deserted chalet on the other side of the Maritime Alps. Who they were going to meet, Isabelle hadn't discovered, but had carried out all the necessary preparations to François' detail.

The distant drone of his motor bike told her that her waiting was soon to be over.

Clambering the balcony, François was pleased to note her readiness, until the beam of his torch struck a tray. "What's this?" he bellowed, "We haven't time for coffee". Isabelle turned to reply, "Inspector Brûlot requested some, he couldn't think of anything more appropriate".

A drink to grace any festivity and a preparation to endear
the gourmet soul. Merging slightly spiced and fruity
flavours over the palate, *Café Brûlot* will also bring a fresh
alternative to your aprés–ski sessions.

Serves Two

In a tiny saucepan, gently heat four table-spoons of
cognac, two of *Cointreau*, two tea-spoons of brown sugar,
four cloves, two strips each of lemon and orange-peel and
a two-inch stick of cinnamon. Allow to simmer lightly for
about 45 seconds to activate the flavours, then remove the
solid ingredients and set the remaining mixture alight.
Immediately pour into the espressos, which need to have
been prepared in slightly larger cups. Await the most
delightful of aromas, before the crescendo of taste.

Café Brûlot

Shades McCloy, a moderately successful jazz pianist from Chicago had for many years sought that individual sound, which if he was ever to achieve recognition as an all time great, would have been instrumental.

His prolonged quest, experimenting with various pianos, amplification and sound systems had rendered him penniless. These debts were soon to be compounded by the arrival of yet another upright, this time imported from a specialist in Europe.

On receipt, his anticipation of joy rapidly disintegrated, leaving Shades with a bad case of the blues. His depression spurning a volley of transatlantic expletives to the supplier. Reluctantly it was agreed to take the piano back.

To arrest his flagging spirits, shades fixed himself a bracing coffee and cognac cocktail, and approached the now partly crated piano.

With casual attention he began to play the opening bars to one of his favourite arrangements. At once, ears agog and heart a-flutter, that laid back mellow sound which had eluded him for so long emerged from the crate.

At last fame was in his grasp.

Into a medium-sized tumbler drop sufficient ice to fill the
glass, add a sweetened espresso and swirl to chill. Pour in
a compliment of cognac, measured to taste, then stir in
cold milk to just below the rim. A thirst-slaking drink
and music to the taste buds.

Shades Delight

RECIPE INDEX

Algerian Coffee Store Ltd., 52 Old Compton Street, London W1V 6PB. Tel: 071 437 2480.

A mecca for coffee lovers. A wide variety of coffees and an excellent range of equipment, including grinders.

Boodles Trading Company, 1 Dial Lane, Ipswich, Suffolk. Tel: 0473 254241.

Own roast and ground coffees only, also available by mail order. Stockists of Gaggia domestic espresso machines.

Brasilia (UK) Ltd., Unit 3, 22 Bull lane, London N18 1RA. Tel: 081 807 4654.

Sole importers of Brasilia espresso machines and grinders from Italy. For more information on sales contact Louie Salvoni or Andy Pugh.

The Coffee Connection Co. Ltd., Unit 14, The Edge Business Centre, Humber Road, London NW2 6EW. Tel: 081 208 0041.

Importers and distributors of the domestic range of Gaggia espresso machines and grinders.

The Coffee Shop, 58 King Street, Cambridge, Cambs. Tel: 0223 358005.

Two outlets, the second is in Oxford. Own brand roast and ground coffee and sales of espresso machines and stove-top pots.

Daria's, 8 County Arcade, Leeds, Yorkshire. Tel: 0532 465598.

Sales of coffee, but no equipment or mail order service. Stockists of Flavor-Mate coffee flavourings.

Drury Lane Tea & Coffee Co. Ltd., 37 Drury Lane, London WC2. Tel: 071 836 2607

Three outlets in London, one in Brighton. Own brand roast and ground coffee and a very good selection of equipment and accessories. They are also able to supply commercial machines. Mail order service.

Fairfax Engineering Ltd., 1 Regency Parade, Swiss Cottage, London NW3 5EQ. Tel: 071 722 7648.

Importers and distributors of the La Pavoni domestic range of espresso machines.

L. Fern & Co. Ltd., 27 Rathbone Place, Oxford Street, London W1P 2EP. Tel: 071 636 2237.

Sales of their own roast and ground coffee, also equipment and accessories.

H. R. Higgins Ltd., 79 Duke Street, London W1M 6AS. Tel: 071 629 3913.

Own brand roast and ground coffee. They offer the *Creole* blend for espresso. Sales of equipment includes domestic espresso makers. Mail order service.

Importers (Head Office Only), Unit 19, North Orbital Trading Estate, Mapsbury Lane, St Albans, Herts. Tel: 0727 42229

17 outlets in the UK. Own extensive range and blends of roast and ground coffee including one branded '*Espresso*'. Sales of domestic machines, stove-top pots and crockery. Mail order service.

Lavazza Coffee (UK) Ltd., Swan Centre, 4 The Courtyard, Fishers Lane, London W4 1RX. Tel: 081 994 6382.

Importers and distributors of one of the proprietary brands of pre-packed roast and ground espresso coffees. The range generally available in the UK includes:

CAFFÈ ESPRESSO

A 100% arabica blend with a sweet and smooth flavour.

QUALITA ROSSA

A leading espresso brand in Italy. A strong and robust coffee.

QUALITA ORO

A blend of arabicas giving a full bodied taste and aroma.

DEK

Naturally decaffeinated espresso coffee, 100% arabica. The first decaf. espresso coffee in the UK.

Most blends are available at good delicatessens and independent coffee retailers, with the Caffè Espresso and Qualita Rossa widely on sale at leading supermarkets.

Lavazza (UK) also import the *Principessa* 4 cup espresso stove-top pot and the *Miss Lavazza* 4 and 6 cup espresso stove-top pot.

Mansfield Marketing Company, 15 Glebe View, Woodhall Park, Mansfield, Notts., NG19 0QE. Tel: 0623 650828.

Importers of Flavor-Mate coffee flavourings from the USA. A wide choice of 12 flavours are available and include, Amaretto, Orange-Cappuccino, Irish Cream and Chocolate Almond.

Markus Coffee Company Ltd., 13 Connaught Street, London W2 2AY. Tel: 071 723 4020.

Own brand coffees only and a good range of domestic espresso machines. Mail order available.

Pitkin & Ruddock, Unit 1, Capital Estate, Whapload Road, Lowestoft, Suffolk. Tel: 0502 563629.

One of ten distributors in the UK for La Cimbali espresso machines. For further information or sales contact Tim Howes.

Pollards Ltd., 2-4 Charles Street, Sheffield, Staffs. Tel: 0742 725460.

Two branches in the Sheffield area selling their own brand coffee as well as other proprietary brands. They also sell espresso machines and stove-top pots as well as Flavor–Mate coffee flavourings. Mail order service available.

St James Street Delicatessen, St James Street, Derby, Derbyshire. Tel: 0332 31255

Mainly a gourmet delicatessen, selling pre-ground vacuum packed Italian coffee. They will also grind coffee to customers specifications, and offer a range of stainless-steel stove pots.

The Tea & Coffee Shop, 4 Arcade Walk, Hitchin, Herts. FG5 1EE. Tel: 0462 433631.

A good selection of pre-packed coffees, as well as coffee ground to your own choice. They are about to launch their own range entitled, 'Something Special'. Sales of equipment and accessories. Mail order service available.

Whittard of Chelsea, 73 Northcote Road, London SW11 6PJ. Tel: 071 924 1888.

Over 20 outlets in the UK. Excellent source for both roast and ground coffee as well as brewing equipment and accessories. Extensive mail order service. Stockists of Flavor–Mate coffee flavouring.

NB. *Most Italian delicatessens will grind their own coffee as well as offer other proprietary brands such as Lavazza and Segafredo. Many sell stove-top pots and a limited number of outlets will also stock domestic espresso machines.*

Aroma, 1b Dean Street, London W1. Tel: 071 287 1633

A café bar with an altogether vivacious ambiance. Great espresso
cuisine, (Aroma actually have a coffee menu) as well as gourmet
'sarnies' and served by dedicated staff all to a backdrop of
Latin-American rhythms. You can also buy coffee, stove-pots,
as well as coffee crockery.

Bar Italia, 22 Frith Street, London W1V. Tel: 071 437 4520

To our knowledge the only authentic Italian espresso bar in London.
Excellent Italian espresso and cappuccino as well as snacks. If you
like Italian football with an atmosphere to boot, Bar Italia have
a giant TV screen to relay the action. They also sell coffee for
home espresso.

Davids, Kenneth, *The Coffee Book*
(U.K., Weybridge, Surrey, Whittet Books Ltd, 1980)

A most informative and marvellously entertaining book, and one of our inspirations. The book contains a very good section on espresso.

Roden, Claudia, *Coffee*
(London, Penguin Books 1986)

The only book on coffee, we found on general sale in London. More on the surface rather than in depth and some very good recipes.